# Seasons
of Damage
and Beauty

Paul Surman

**Seasons of Damage and Beauty**

© Paul Surman

First Edition 2021

has asserted their authorship and given their permission to Dempsey & Windle for these poems to be published here.

All rights reserved. No part of this publication may be reproduced, stored in a retrieval system or transmitted in any form or by any means without the written consent of the author, nor otherwise circulated in any form of binding or cover other than that in which it is published and without a similar condition being imposed on a subsequent purchaser.

Published by Dempsey & Windle under their VOLE imprint.

15 Rosetrees
Guildford
Surrey
GU1 2HS
UK
01483 571164
dempseyandwindle.com

British Library Cataloguing-in-Publication Data

A catalogue record for this book is available from the British Library

ISBN: 978-1-913329-40-2

Printed and bound In the United Kingdom

for Christine with love

## Acknowledgements

Some of these poems, or versions of them, have previously been published in Acumen, Dream Catcher, Fire, Prole, South, and The Journal.

I would like to acknowledge the help and friendship of the members of Back Room Poets in Oxford.

**Poems**

| | |
|---|---:|
| First Light | 11 |
| Life is a Story We Tell Ourselves by Being Sentient | 12 |
| Buoys | 13 |
| The Day | 14 |
| Seeing the Angel | 15 |
| Remote Sensing | 16 |
| Nameless | 17 |
| Rain in the Night | 18 |
| Before Nightfall | 19 |
| Altered States | 20 |
| The Fall | 21 |
| Vapour Trails | 22 |
| Epiphany | 23 |
| Everything is Wrong | 24 |
| Blackbird | 25 |
| Elsewhere | 26 |
| Street Lamp | 27 |
| Crow Time | 28 |
| Spring | 29 |
| Rural | 30 |
| Intervals | 31 |
| Conifer | 32 |
| Porter | 33 |
| Alarm Call | 34 |
| Roots | 35 |
| Horses | 36 |
| Wren | 37 |

| | |
|---|---|
| Murmuration Over Otmoor | 38 |
| Mislaid | 39 |
| Bird Skull | 40 |
| After Nightfall | 41 |
| That's the way to do it | 42 |
| The Mood I'm In | 43 |
| Some Stars | 44 |
| The Meaning of Life | 45 |
| Glitch | 46 |
| In Outer Space | 47 |
| Distances | 48 |
| Walking | 49 |
| A Squirrel on the Footpath Between Rockwell End and Colstrope – Chilterns | 50 |
| Starlings | 51 |
| Birdsong in Winter | 52 |
| Night | 53 |
| It is | 54 |
| The Hour | 55 |
| Rooks | 56 |
| Philosophy | 57 |
| Late Summer | 58 |
| Moon Gazing | 59 |
| Invisible | 60 |

*Brief is this existence, as a visit in a strange house. The path to be pursued is poorly lit by a flickering consciousness.*

Albert Einstein

## FIRST LIGHT

In this state you are both king and outcast.
The house is dangerous at first light,
neither dream nor consciousness
and at daggers drawn, its walls and rooms
are calmly psychological, quietly deranged.

Your thoughts stumble on a dark turn
of the rational stair, and you fall, pitched forward
through a mirrored curve in the concave air
towards inefficient reality.

You wake! The soft explosion of eyes open,
as if a needle's weightless flicker records
the slight electric of a life, its soundless click.

The aftermath of yesterday restarts time,
complex diagrams are drawn again from scratch.

## LIFE IS A STORY WE TELL OURSELVES
## BY BEING SENTIENT

The terrible fascination of being alive
in a primitive world still violent
with contradictions, this ghostly home

draped with the fluttering shapes
of torn imaginings. Seasons of damage
and beauty, of enlightenment

and opposition. Storms sweeping in,
like an inquisitor who shakes the trees.
Day sauntering from light to dark

and back again, our meandering path
that will not free us or explain itself.
The wood I walked in after dark

that led to these forsaken fields where
a soft light from the sky rests tenderly.

**BUOYS**

From the vantage point of a mind, to feel
the loneliness of isolated objects. Afloat
in wakefulness you can understand buoys

slung beneath the cold enclosure of night,
lurching on a burly tide, secured but adrift
in a close to abstract curve of the bay.

Touched by a scarce light; lifted up, cast
down, they survive, their numbers
and letters a charm against gaping fathoms.

They mark an exact position in the anxious
momentum of the waves, as we ride out
long hours in the weather of our thoughts.

## THE DAY

You have to imagine it or it won't come true.
A day of beauty you will know of in advance
when the air trembles then slows to a graceful halt,
and the landscape seems to look you in the eye.

You can feel its intelligence of hills and distances,
and something closer, as if it is seeing through
your skin, so close you are sure it must be asking
the question to which you alone are the answer.

Now you are both daylight and darkness. Strong
as a sapling, and weak as thunder. Your breath
light as the soil, heavy as air. Your blood
elated in its echoing passageways. Your thoughts
no longer separate from the world you have known
as it reaches in to touch you, very softly.

## SEEING THE ANGEL

It might have arrived
out of a tangle of background detail:
the roses already going over
at the end of summer, the garden
sprawling towards decay.

If it were possible at all,
it would be at one of those times
in a life when you are no longer
exactly who you were, but not yet
who you will become.

Perhaps a disorderly breeze would
tousle an unkempt sky over the dying
garden—a breath of disquiet,
movement breaking things apart
with an unsettling vision.

It will be standing there then,
made from the tall spaces between
organic forms, forsythia and the like.
From the prodigious earth,
a wingless, irreligious angel.

Not the angel of cold perfection
and vatic pronouncement. But one
of absence and imperfection, real
in the way that voids between words
allow them to make sense.

## REMOTE SENSING

Waking in the night I might go anywhere.
My mind is a cursor blink,
awaiting commands.

*I type instructions on an invisible keyboard.*

And I am a motorway camera, looking down,
unblinking on a hairline fracture
in the wideness of the night.

I am consciousness leaping from camera
to camera. Observing objectively
night's deliveries lumbering through.

I am vacant spaces in service station
car parks, emptiness divided up
into landscapes of white lines.

*I hit escape, and tap once more*
*on the numb letters of night's keyboard*

Now I'm on the Ridgeway's ancient track,
fearful at every turn or crossing, as shadows
ambush shadows in the dark.

Things merge or collude, vanish or appear,
or were never there; they listen
to my breathing, the noise my mind makes.

I reach the neolithic at Wayland's Smithy
and peer into its far chamber where time
and darkness are curled asleep.

**NAMELESS**

Under a late autumn morning sky
I need a word for a moment
that is neither dark nor light.
Not so much a time of day
as a hesitation of being.

Twilight or crepuscular can't describe
the mood I'm in at times like this,
when walking to the village shop
for a pint of milk or a newspaper
I am overflown by red kites.
Dark shapes, fork-tailed cut-outs,
made from leftovers of the night.

A stealthy feeling rises through me,
instinctual as ancestor worship; I know
there should be a name for it,
but there isn't.

## RAIN IN THE NIGHT

Soft as kindness,
rain falls lightly
on summer gardens.

Is this the sound
oblivion makes?
Its gentle insistence
comforts me,

speaks in whispers
of life still to live
beyond these formless,
sleepless hours.

Blind clouds sent rain
to search the land.
Hearing it I know
the world's still there.

A shadow-me rises,
goes out, stumbles
through wet grass
in our local fields

where the horses whinny
to see me out so late
in my dark disguise.

## BEFORE NIGHTFALL

The evening's eyelids droop, it can hardly stay awake
as it tries to write a note to the night
about the day's events.

The washing line, arms folded away under its cover,
looks like an exclamation mark. It tries
to remember what it is there to emphasise,
but fails, so falls asleep.

A bat arrives, swerves and flutters,
like a niggling thought at the back of the garden's mind,
but unable to jog its memory, flits into forgetfulness.

Two garden chairs, companionably side by side,
are sure their services won't be needed
now that the light is fading, the air is growing chill,
so sit back in themselves, and take their ease.

## ALTERED STATES

The sodium fox was a statue of itself
in the street lights unquiet light.
Not magic, but magical.

Then the glamour of its bright
electric motion as it ran into the dark.
No need to be more than what it is.

No need for a world more
beautiful and perfect than the one
it owned by being there.

It disappeared into my thoughts,
leaving its strong but elusive odour
across uneven cognitive fields.

I lost it there, but its blur
was with me for days as my mind
invented a continuing story.

I could spend a lifetime tracking it
and never find it again, changed
to the colour of moonlight or dream.

**THE FALL**

From within the long black factory of sleep—
where the mind clocks on to
a Punch and Judy night-shift,
to flounder and rejoice in its own rawness,
its sacred violence, and brute tenderness—
blind, you leap across a blank abyss

to an altered state where daylight is,
that questions everything with reality's
unprincipled stare. But what if you had missed
your footing, slipped into the numb crevasse
between sleeping and waking, where a god lives,
cold-eyed, abstract?

**VAPOUR TRAILS**

I like to think of them as graffiti by a vast
invisibility, who, latent with excess of power
could easily smash the sky in, leaving just

another broken window, but instead it scores
a thin bright scratch in the cerulean bodywork
of air—the kind of thing you might expect

of a god with time on its hands: secretive being
so naked it can't be seen. This morning it makes
a criss-cross pattern, etched in the acid yellow

of the early sun, then bored with that, allows it
to fade, loosen, fall apart like a dress undone,
exposing once more the bare original of blue.

I sensed it was pleased with this, its trick
of change, but you can never tell with a god,
whose fleeting thoughts can scorch the earth

by accident, set trees aflame, make riverbanks
collapse, cause hailstorm or tempest; with a flicker
of eyelids send flash floods, or dirty tides

racing for the coast to flush the land of humans:
but look at it now, this god of terrible destruction
repeating this same detail like a mind obsessed.

## EPIPHANY

Do not disturb me. I am in conference
with the day. In urgent discussion with
a passing car, the postman on his round,
a finch sitting longer than expected

on a lilac branch, as if in quiet thought.
I am taking my place in the ordinary,
enjoying the knowable limits of what is.
For a moment everything is in stasis.

Then off it goes again, the astonishingly
usual, getting on with being part of life,
untroubled by its meaning or the truth.
The car's sound diminishing on its way,

the finch flying off, the rattle and clank
of the letterbox as post flops onto the mat.

## EVERYTHING IS WRONG

*'I almost think we are all of us ghosts'*
                     *Henrik Ibsen*

You can't understand it. Everything—
just as it was. The window still projects
a skewed version of its shape onto the lawn,
framing the inner light of home.

The garden's deep shade is, as usual,
inhospitable, ominous night-sky black,
and furtiveness is the rule
among trees and shrubs.

You stand in the house's throwaway light
that crash-lands silently around you,
but don't notice that you cast no shadow.

Why do you feel so absent from yourself?

You want to return to familiar rooms,
but the door handle can't be grasped
or turned. It's as if the locks
have been changed against you.

Looking in at the window you are snubbed.
Your knocks upon the glass are worryingly
ineffectual. How will they recognise you
if they don't look back?

You realise you don't know what year it is,
or what happened before this moment.
Looking up at stars you understand vastness;
that nothing matters, or ever has.

**BLACKBIRD**

You have been there for a while now,
perched in the lilac, poised
between arrival and departure,
beautifully undecided in the branches,
where fresh green leaves
and spikes of purple flowers
surround you.

The day was dark, the evening
looks haggard in the rain.
You are taking time to think,
head moving from side to side,
tilted at an angle, as if inclined to doubt.
But believe me, the world is only real
because of the brightness of your beak.

**ELSEWHERE**

I know this village, but don't
know exactly where it is. And why
it is only ever high summer there,
or wintry Christmas.

I know its love affairs and murders.
I have laid a hand against
the warmth of its walls, and waded
for hours in the cool of its stream.

I'm familiar with the chaos of its
birdsong; its distant shouts, laughter
and lawnmowers; private sighs,
bell-sounds and silences.

Above all other sounds I know
the sound of the bell on the door
of the village shop, with its jangle
of entrance and departure.

I have lived forever in the village's
half-dreamt of sunlight; observed
shadows stretched across its streets
or leaning idly against house fronts.

I know its history better than anyone.
Past lives of publican or ploughmen.
The ghosts of its manor house.
I am their myth as they are mine.

**SPRING**

The spring waits for us in empty rooms
on the other side of time, rooms that no one
ever visits, or lives in. I feel as if I'm there,
thinking thoughts I hardly know as mine.

Or it's beyond high walls I cannot see over.
Yet I seem to know the colours and textures
of the days there, that I have not lived through
and may never know. I can see Dog's Mercury
along woodland paths. Star-shaped Celandines
alive in hedgerows at the back of winter,
in a landscape nobody owns, and where snow
won't ever have fallen. I walk towards spring
on raw winter evenings, through weather
that is my own, where footsteps fall unheard.

**RURAL**

I am a silence on which birds
write a graffiti of songs
that I erase so they may scrawl
their obsession down again
on a clean sheet of air.

I am a great barn yawning
in midday heat; in my shade
a pile of tractor tyres sleep,
and a dog scratches itself.

I am an isolated cottage
in an extended conversation
with time, a lone citizen
harmonious with its landscape.

I am a village you might find
in the valley when you emerge
from the shade of woods.
A handsome disorderliness
at the centre of the universe.

I am and am not the truth,
just a pale ghost sitting
in a far distant field, my back
to woods as I watch the crops.
You too may sit here one day,
for reasons I won't understand.

## INTERVALS

Time is a table and chair.
You may sit at them to write
perhaps, the poems of life's
seductive archetypes.

Oak trees experience time
differently to us. You feel
their seconds must be large
and sonorous. But in time

an oak may become a table
and chair at which someone
who is just like you may sit
to write the poems of a life.

People, poems, tables, chairs
are notes in time's fugue.
Appear at different intervals
through which time passes.

It is the intervals that matter,
not the man, or the shadow
of a man, but absence walking
featureless between them

like music you cannot hear
as you sit at a table and chair
writing the poems of a life,
a beautiful music of illusion.

## CONIFER

I have cut the great dark conifer down,
where wood pigeons came to rest
unsteadily in the evening, foolishly
rocking to and fro.

I've cut it down, and now it's only logs
and brashings, the great dark conifer
where, of an evening, a robin rested
to warble its song.

But I have cut it down; it had to go.
It was too big, and far too dark, and cast
its gloom, all day and in the evening,
when the birds came.

So I cut the great dark conifer down,
leaving only air where it used to stand,
sombre and unforgiving. Don't be afraid,
come closer, birds. Sing for me.

**PORTER**

Dear esteemed village brewer.
I know you are a wise man
because I've tasted the wisdom
in your beer, and wanted more.

I know you will have noticed
that even the leaves still green,
look hesitant now as they once
were noisily bright and certain.

It's that time of year people stand
at their back doors to see night
walking early, but funereally slow
from the far end of the garden.

A cortège of darkness and stars
moving slack-faced and solemn
behind it, with the slow drum
of winter following on.

I think you know what I want,
serious beer for a serious season.
Old man's beer of quiet thought,
a case of your excellent porter.

**ALARM CALL**

I lie awake, waiting to hear the first bird
give the arrival of dawn the official consent
of its song.

              Its plumage
is of no particular colour. The colour
of the night perhaps, that great gallimaufry
of the sleeping and the sleepless.

The colour of the individual
and the universal. The colour of the nation
of sleep, its dreams combined.
The bird doesn't worry about such things,
and is not awed by its coming task.
Knows that the perfect time for it to sing
is when it sings.

              That everyone, awake
or asleep, waits for daylight, sure that one way
or another it will overwhelm them.

**ROOTS**

He might be human, might be myth;
newly deposed king, lover fresh from the wrong
person's bed, or simple unfortunate
with dangerous genes and chaotic life.

Far behind hurtles a pack of yelping dogs,
followed by an undisciplined human rabble, colliding
and falling over each other like hapless cops
in a silent movie chase.

His shirt flaps wildly as he tramples through crops,
but he's quick as a shadow sliding off walls.
The day is hot, his scent grows stronger;
it's certain the dogs will sniff him out.

Ivory highlights in dark curly hair
could be horns peeking through. Do his
trouserless, hairy legs end in hooves? He's fast,
but trots unsteadily as if trying to run in high heels.

There they are, deep and dark inviting woods.
Although he can't see past them, when the trees
close around him he's not obscured;
gaps between trunks can be seen right through.

What to do? He thinks he must become a tree:
stands there stiffly, sends down roots; he must
be mythical because he's sprouting leaves.
His pursuers chase on by, unaware that man

is the myth he thinks. Now they've gone, nerves
become calm as ancient flutes. But a laggard dog,
stops and sniffs, raises a leg. Can dogs smile?
He pisses all over our hero's lower branches.

## HORSES

Don't spare the horses, as they say:
those sleek monsters.
Ride them hard and fast, as if,
hair draggled, shirt untucked,
pockets stuffed with someone else's
cash, you are escaping
with whole counties in pursuit.

Don't worry about what century it is;
keep going until stars
needle your thoughts,
and your horse snorts loudly with
triumph or exhaustion.

They would only have spent the day
in a field listlessly swishing their tail,
bitten by flies that made broad flanks
shudder. Shoving their great head
over a hedge so that anyone
might stroke their muzzle.

When it started to get dark, part
by equine part, withers to fetlock,
they would have disappeared
into the surrounding darkness,
as if they had become mythical.

## WREN

The kitchen window was hardly open
when you flew in
                and were lost
in a world that had changed to walls
and unreliable air.

I think you must have been a ghost.
I saw your chestnut-coloured softness,
but when I held you in my hands
you were not there.

The hardly anything weight of you
made weightless seem more plausible,
in the way that almost nothing
can appear substantial. As if the idea of you
was playing at being supernatural.

Our mutual anxiety was my only burden.
As I put you down on the garden table
you trembled and shook.
For however long it took, I kept watch.

Whole ages passed in the insignificance
of this somewhere in eternity. When you
shuddered I thought you must be dying.

Then you looked nervously around
as if in tiny astonishment
at everything you saw. Long minutes passed

until, on your thin-as-grass-stems legs,
you turned into an insubstantial phoenix,
a slightness that knew its way.

## MURMURATION OVER OTMOOR

Everyone stands along a grassy bank and stares,
as if at the blank expression of time passing.
Then they are there, dark dots, avian punctuation.

From a concealed opening in the sky they flick, twist,
roll, fold; the air allows this to happen, doesn't interfere
as they darken, lighten, attenuate and thicken.

More appear: warp, skew, and in a vast gasp
expand, implode, until with kamikaze abandon,
as if they had been syphoned there,
flock after flock hurtles at the ground.

Between the reeds and the stolid church tower
of a distant village, the sharp sound
of their voices speckles unseen ground,
and with every fall to earth the din intensifies,
becoming fluid as the sound of fast-flowing water.

Magic show over, we turn to walk away.
You won't believe me, but as we walk a half-moon
strips the trees bare with its x-ray sight,
and in an occult atmosphere, cows moo tunefully
in unison, and as light fades over the misty earth
a last soft glimmer dies, extinguishing everything.

## MISLAID

Walking the street's simple idyll
I pass a dry-cleaner's, avoid the green
bicycle leant against a lamp post, smile
at a large man holding a small dog,
its eyes alert under an excess of fur.

I look into the plate glass shop front's
reality, where the real floats thinly
on glass and daylight, mixing inner
and outer, moment and eternity,
to become lost, like me, in a glance.

I look into a barber shop and know
how it feels to be the gowned patient
in the chair, watching the barber's neat
choreography, as he moves elegantly
to perform his minor operation.

I like to think of myself as someone else,
who, walking ahead of me, disappears
around a corner, and is gone, quick
as split seconds into history, eluding
infinity's dangerously impartial smile.

**BIRD SKULL**

I found his head
beneath a tree, wrapped
in the last of its skin,
leaf-like but leathery.

Imagined his final flight,
a cold sky behind his eyes;
world without landmark
or destination, abiding fear
of his aviator's mind.

The tree he rested in was
part of him, heavy and still;
his blood like the blood
of the branches, ran
slow and resinous
beneath each feather.

Light faded
in a diminishing sky
still pulsing with the song
of his kind, their sound
arriving fast and thin,
lost electricity earthed
in him, in his eyelids'
final flicker. The sky
soared about him as he fell.

**AFTER NIGHTFALL**

I love the calm feel at the close of certain days.
When I take the dog out for her to sniff
the air and have a pee, and she
rushes out and barks at whatever it is
that is not there. The evening doesn't care.

And every time, I bring back with me
something of the sky—some small thing
that will fit inside the finite mind
to remind me before I sleep of the immensity
in which I am about to dream.

Something near—an aircraft's winking light.
Or far—the vagueness of the milky way.
I might see an omen, say a shooting star
that slashes at the sky with brief significance,
denoting nothing more than peace.

## THAT'S THE WAY TO DO IT

On old stone slabs outside
the ancient library, sits Mr Punch,
or someone uncannily like him
in a tweed jacket, brown felt hat,
a rich red tie neatly knotted,
and bright yellow corduroy
trousers. In the flesh he seems
as real as unreality often does.

He's playing the role of much loved
character actor, relaxing
between performances. You suspect
that if recognized he will let loose
with a burst of his famous acting,
repeating catch phrases, but falling
well short of actual violence,
then smiling amiably. What lies
behind his eyes are thoughts
so sinister that even he can't bear
to let them linger in the mind
for long. When they do it's as if
he is the whole cast: the baby,
constable, clown and crocodile;
skeleton, doctor, and even Judy,
all of them in terrifying motion.

## THE MOOD I'M IN

I have known many flooded fields,
heard so much laughter after dark.
Things I've woven together as best I could
to make a story in which I've spent my time
making elegies out of events.

Everything is made of passing thoughts,
so I step back into the alley's gloom,
clutching my suitcase as if what it contains
will carry me away like heavy traffic,
along scalded roads to another town.

Sunlight falls differently somewhere else;
shadows are back to front, or so it seems
when who I was is a story I made up,
and who I am is where I'm going now.

**SOME STARS**

Sorcery of tinsel or hydrogen engines.
The drawing room door is closed
and walls are a disinterested darkness
the window is suspended in.

Walls and window are only an image
in the cosmological vastness of the mind;
I travel past who I am to where
ambiguity is the only reality.

My face touches the great emptiness;
starlight passes through my flesh.
I imagine myself a limitless equation
concerning all that is, and isn't.

Neither fully actual nor entirely notional,
I look through the window at some stars.

## THE MEANING OF LIFE

It is the ordinariness of the ordinary.
The supermarket van on its round,
with its ugly beauty of everyday alive.

It is that, and more—much more.
It is the pizza delivery moped
with its huge square box on the back.

It is precisely that. Its loveliness,
not the loveliness of loins and grace,
or the promise after promise

of something better. It's the sheer excess
of the lorry carrying an overloaded skip,
its rattles and clanks. It is that too.

It is sunshine on the stink of things.
It is the stink of being alive. Yes.

## GLITCH

*After Francis Bacon*

I am stuck at the screaming edge of visible,
a spacial uncertainty, in a place made
mostly of time, where a see-through self
tries to imagine what it is to exist.

Without coherent shape, colour, shoe or collar size,
my blurred and shifting body
is made from inconsistencies of the mind.
Flickers between states like an electrical fault.

Part of a notional arm or foot dissolves into air,
vanishes through earth. Nothing is entirely solid,
and I am neither missing nor found,
only about to become, or not.

I mustn't stay too long like this. It's ghostly here
and, see, it's already dark, of which I am a part.

## IN OUTER SPACE

As usual, philosophy is useless
but important. How weightless we are
without the old idea of soul
to hold us down.

The capsule, real to touch,
appears to be made from a dream.
Truth suspended hauntingly
between tangible and ethereal.

We know it's a long way to go
before our disembodied footprints
become graphic proof
we walked on soundless acres.

So we speak to an almost notional earth,
which talks back in a calm
cracked voice. But on a journey
you think about the journey.

Life, after all, is always an unstable mix
of maths and romance. Here
you think of the self as the poem
of what you do. So you settle down

to pass through colourless time,
fixed on the routines you learned,
half-watching the meaningless stars
as you keep a check on instruments.

**DISTANCES**

We can't hear, as Cassini did, the lifeless howl of Saturn,
can only reach out imagined distance-traversing arms
into the darkness of seven hundred million miles.

But it is too far to feel our hands touch or explore
the ghost of radio emissions of what we want to know
in the out-there-somewhere of an imperfect vacuum,
with its solar winds and sleeves of space dust.

We can't feel asteroids fall light as an idea on the skin
of our phantom arms stretched across barren star fields,
the backdrop to an emptiness in which imagination
suffocates in wide-openness endlessly continuing.

Here we'd be annihilated by perfect terror in isolation
where space and time flow unchecked towards infinity,
and distances in all dimensions destroy us and our gods.

**WALKING**

*for Christine*
*14 February, 1998.*

Winter shadows stretch across a lane,
a plane drones a reminder of summer,
willows live in unison with a stream,
calves in a byre sit on straw amazed.

We come and go by ways commonplace
as folklore, quietly so we do not wake
the ancient villages we pass, churches
hushed into place by centuries of praise.

But we sense a different world of power,
a pagan silence stored in solitary barns:
the curiosity of cattle, a barn owl flying
on muted wings between two woods.

## A SQUIRREL ON THE FOOTPATH BETWEEN ROCKWELL END AND COLSTROPE – CHILTERNS

The gape of delicate jaws
like a breathless gasp, eyes
a wide-open blankness.
It still wore its lovely pelt.

Its clock had stopped,
but the flow remained
in its fur, the something
sleek in it that had once
given unexpected grace
to the follow-me-quick
lift and lurch of its tail.

But no tiny watch-like
tick of the heart, propelled
a minimal flow of blood.

The vivid head to tail of it
was a dead and alive
contradiction, until you saw
one leg still in the trap
it couldn't shake off,
exhibit A in the evidence
for the prosecution.

## STARLINGS

They have pointy heads, quarrelsome ways,
dark aspects that, close-up, shimmer
like flocks in the sky, with a sheen
of purple and green. They sing

from a scribbled manuscript of avian equations.
A saucy song of innuendos,
prequels and sequels, of nothing much
about everything that is.

They've a language of rattles, clicks, whistles,
and dirty chuckles scrawled on air,
that reaches jauntily down to us
from chimney pots and trees.

It's the song of thousands of their kind,
much the same as ours, starting
where it starts, and ending where it ends,
life within limits.

It sounds like everything and anything;
a radio not tuned in, rowdiness, telephones,
wayward jazz, a kind of manifesto.
The way they tell it, this is what being alive is.

## BIRDSONG IN WINTER

I know that blank yellow rectangle
is a high window, expressionless except
for an even light that feels symbolic of calm
to a mind always craving order.

In the early morning dark, the slant of the roof
from which it bestows its easeful simplicity,
might only be there to provide context
to the window's understated secular magic.

I continue my descent of the familiar hill's
latest uncertainties, passing under street lights
at the centre of a transformational eeriness—
houses hidden in the darkness of their shapes.

A cat crosses the road's dirty luminescence,
with that steady self-confidence of motion
with which it has stalked, without remorse,
the distant corners of the night's unholiness.

At the hill's foot it happens. A blackbird sings
its rich melodious song that repairs even
that which is not broken. Across obscure fields
unseen birds start singing in disorderly unison.

**NIGHT**

is coming into view, like an old friend
deep in thought, ambling dreamily
out of the undomesticated land.

Black wings are folded away
inside a tree's cold shelter, with caws
of quarrelsome settling down.

Now the night, lost in its glances,
frowns, and gloomy intentions, idles
solemnly along garden paths.

It stops to look under bushes, then
slides beneath them to where the garden
is slowly forgetting its deaths.

And I am ready to turn away
from evening's peace and disquiet,
to wait out the hours in secluded rooms,

to extinguish lights and turn towards
sleep, leaving the night to its hoots,
scurries and squeals. Its long silences.

**IT IS**

the blackbird's final phrase of the day.
It is a crow admonished by silence.

It is the erratic freedom of moths
flourishing prior to the flight of bats.

It is night descending slowly
down the levels of the air
to the ground floor of evening,
where a door opens and a fox steps out
to slink along the backs of gardens
dispensing darkness.

It is the imperceptible garment of the air,
never fashionable nor unfashionable.

It is not yet the acceptable corruption
of moonlight on the dark slant of roofs.

It is the simplest expression of what is.
It is past, present, and what happens next

It is me sitting late into my life
hoping for more evenings like this.

**THE HOUR**

Is he winter, this stranger
keeping close to the wood's edge
in the last minutes of light?

His face is troublingly imprecise.
There is something in his frown
that reminds me of weather.

I'm certain his hastening on
has a purpose that's close to him
as thoughts I cannot guess at.

He stops, and stands becalmed,
as if listening without breath
for something I will never hear.

This is the stillness of invisibility,
and I see that he was, after all,
only the wind quickening in trees.

Without a glance at me, he'll be
gone before I see him go, as rain
falls lightly at first, then heavily.

**ROOKS**

Halfway around
and there they are.
They would be white
in negative,
but are dense black
in the here and now
of raw reality's
finished print.
I love the crudity
of their conversation.
Where in reverse,
sound would be silence,
it is now a stark
incarnation of ruin.

I stop to see sunlight
darken them
as I listen to
the harsh congregation
of their voices,
a wilderness of being,
and love them
for their refusal
to tell things better
than they are. Love
their black shine,
and iridescence,
their voices hard
and mineral sharp.

## PHILOSOPHY

That the meaning of life is life
we confirm every day by being alive.

But mind is greedy for something other
than shadow and reflection,
a dappled existence of light and shade.

Wants more than formless clouds,
fleeing across complicit hillsides,
blown by turbulent winds
whose turn and turn about makes
an agile imprint on placid uphill grasslands
panicked into motion.

Wants more even than the lovers, lying
secretly in bracken's antediluvian arms,
as if life's embrace is keeping them hidden
from implacable midday heat of prying eyes.

Wants something greater than a fox
slinking home in early morning light,
happily guilty, at ease with pungent foxiness.

The crops packed tight in fields give cover
to the harvest mouse taking grain
from cereal heads, blunt nose twitching,
small bright eyes. Yet mind wants more.

But what do I know? The mind has little time
for poets and artists, says it requires
philosophers, that it must pin things down.

## LATE SUMMER

The evening has lost its verve,
leaves so quickly now,
increasingly reluctant to remain.

It had seemed to relish
being leisurely, and staying late,
falling asleep by my side.

Enjoyed the effect its perfumes,
and the earthy wantonness
of its sensuality had on me.

Now it has a tendency to shiver,
to pull a face, and without
so much as a muttered excuse,

edges towards a darker corner
of itself, from which it looks
over its shoulder with contempt.

I know it's out of love with me,
and its impatience to be gone
will grow with every passing day.

## MOON GAZING

In imagined primeval landscapes
early humans enter your thoughts.
Don't call them primitive or naive.

Conjure them instead, heads raised
gazing at the phosphorescent silence,
unnerving whiteness of the moon.

Same spirit light as will-o'-the-wisp,
bare and magical, dead that feels alive,
its silence is a slow-burning sound.

The stark radiation of its light upon
our ancestors, split black from bright.
A vision of cataclysmic nakedness.

Looking at moonlight in the present,
its fanatical effects, its biting acid,
drowns reason in annihilating light.

**INVISIBLE**

In my final years, if I am fit enough in winter,
I would like to tend to the needs of a wood
of oak, hazel and ash. To live inside its poem.

I will build a fire for my old dog to sit beside
while I work, and keep my saw and billhook sharp.
Woodsmoke incense will permeate my clothes
as I listen to silence listen to itself.

For years I worked for the makers of money
and strife; now in my final days I will work
for the love of a wood, and life. Use my powers
wisely, and ignore all passers-by, measuring
the hours of the day by progress that I make—
growing quiet and strong to myself.

And where in the last hours of life
I work in the quietest quarter of the wood,
when I have gone, anemones will flower profusely
in spring, and I will never be known again;
except for this flowering and a new season's growth
I will have gone invisibly from the earth.